The People
&
The State

By

Champion Muthle

DEDICATION

For the person I once was.
For all the people who dream of a better life for
themselves and their children, and the leaders who
help them achieve it.

ACKNOWLEDGMENTS

A special thanks to John and Alain Locke, Thomas Jefferson and Benjamin Franklin, Lincoln and FDR, without whom the proper function of the State would still be a mystery.

"Men being...by nature, all free, equal, and independent, no one can be put out of this estate, and subjected to the political power of another, without his own consent. The only way whereby any one divests himself of his natural liberty, and puts on the bonds of civil society, is by agreeing with other men to join and unite into a community for their comfortable, safe, and peaceable living one amongst another, in a secure enjoyment of their properties, and a greater security against any, that are not of it.

But if they have set limits to the duration of their legislative, and made this supreme power in any person, or assembly, only temporary; or else, when by the miscarriages of those in authority, it is forfeited; upon the forfeiture, or at the determination of the time set, it reverts to the society, and the people have a right to act as supreme, and continue the legislative in themselves; or erect a new form, or under the old form place it in new hands, as they think good."

- John Locke, *Second Treatise on Civil Government*

What are the State's responsibilities to the People?
What is the proper function of the State?
These are the questions to which we now turn our attention.

We have come a long way since Thomas Jefferson and Charles Tilly. John Locke and FDR.

But the centrality of the *Social Contract* remains.

Just as all roads lead to Rome, all elements of Government, from the Economy to Health and Human Services, lead back to the Social Contract.

Indeed, the quality and accessibility of the Social Contract is more important than ever before.

But like an outdated and one-sided Service Agreement, the Social Contract has become untenable, invalid, and untrue.

It no longer serves the People, or the Republic.

The quick fixes of Politicians are insufficient and ineffective. We cannot troubleshoot our way out of this mess.

We must begin to envision and deliver a new, more modern Social Contract if the proper functioning of the State is to be achieved, or even set in motion.

This is not a new idea, but the tools and technologies at our disposal are new ones and must be applied correctly.

Government has for too long been concerned with finding *all* the possible ways to support the People, rather than implementing the *utmost effective*, inclusive, and efficient way to do so.

This has led to an excess of ideas and authority, and a dearth of effective action and reform.

This is a process driven by the personal and political preferences, ideologies, inclinations, and temperaments of an elite few, rather than the will of the people.

It is a process beholden not to the People, but rather a small group of political parties.

But the proper function of Government is not a political notion, but rather an Ethical and Moral one. It is not a Democratic or Republican idea, but rather a *Universal* one.

It is an idea that sits at the very core of the future of Civilization, Citizenship, and Society, not the periphery.

The needs of the people are not being met on a grand
and historically significant scale.

The past few decades have seen the Rights and Freedoms of the People reduced, eliminated and restricted more than any other time in our history.

It is true that there are politicians in government who believe it is their right and the right of the State to steal from the People, invade our privacy, deny us justice, and terrorize us.

These politicians must be removed from power as a matter of national and international urgency.

It is also true that in many countries around the world, the People are faced with the most tyrrounous, corrupt, and complacent governments we have ever seen.

24

In these cases, the question of the proper function of Government has yet to even be asked.

These are not insignificant matters.
These are not minor causes for concern.

They are the very foundation upon which our future stands.

If the process of restricting rights continues to be normalized, standardized, and institutionalized in the way that it has, it is not just the People that will suffer, but the entire Planet.

28

I fear we are already well on our way in that direction...the direction of great doom and undoing.

29

We must immediately begin to think, work, and govern against this impending disaster.

And we must do so in a manner that is both authentic and innovative.

Transparency, Accountability, and Progress must be restored to our Government.

We must insist that our Politicians represent the will and meet the demands of all people by and for whom they were elected, not just a select few.

To this end, we must bolster, promote, and prioritize the rights of Minorities, Women and Children, Immigrants, the Poor, and the most vulnerable in our Societies, as well as the best and brightest minds the world has to offer.

34

Again, this is not an insignificant or trifling task. It is, indeed, a moral imperative and the task of our time.

The tools of Technology, Comparative Policy, and Innovation stand at the ready for our disposal, and the People are hungry for progress along these lines.

We have seen the positive power that these forces can have all around the world. Yet we have failed to properly implement them for ourselves.

We seem hell-bent on using these tools for our own destruction and evil ends.

That is the way of disaster and downfall.
That is the way of decline.

Let us, instead, apply the tools of Information, Automation, and Intelligence to our infinite, eternal, and collective rise.

The People, and the Future, demand it.

ABOUT THE AUTHOR

Champion Muthle aka Daniel Maree is an award-winning Writer-Director, Creative and Cultural Strategist, Independent Journalist, Inventor, Philosopher, Creative Technologist, Afro-Futurist, and Social Entrepreneur. He is a Frederick Douglass Scholar and Forbes 30 Under 30 Honoree for Social Entrepreneurship. His work has been featured in the MoMA and the Library of Congress.